THE HANDWRITING
ANALYZER

A useful and entertaining book which puts graphology entirely in the hands of the layman, enabling him to analyze any handwriting quickly and accurately without any study or knowledge of the subject

by Jerome S. Meyer

A FIRESIDE BOOK   Published by Simon and Schuster

Contents

FUNDAMENTALS OF
HANDWRITING ANALYSIS

SITTING opposite you in a bus are two men whom you have never seen before. One is dressed in a bright, checked suit and wears a flashy tie. On his hat is a vivid hatband, and in his lapel a red carnation. The other wears a simple blue serge suit and a subdued tie.

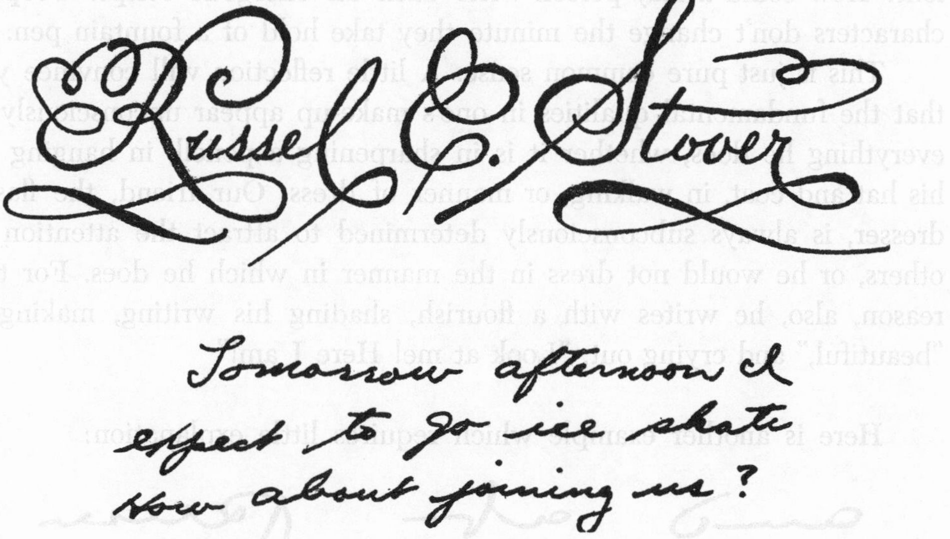

FIGURE 1

Figure 1 shows the handwriting of each man. Would there be any question in your mind which writing belonged to the flashy dresser?

Again, suppose you have advertised for a live-wire salesman, a go-getter and a man who never lets the grass grow under his feet. And suppose you received two letters from applicants, written in their own hand-writing as shown here. Which applicant would you select, the one who wrote specimen A or the one who wrote specimen B?

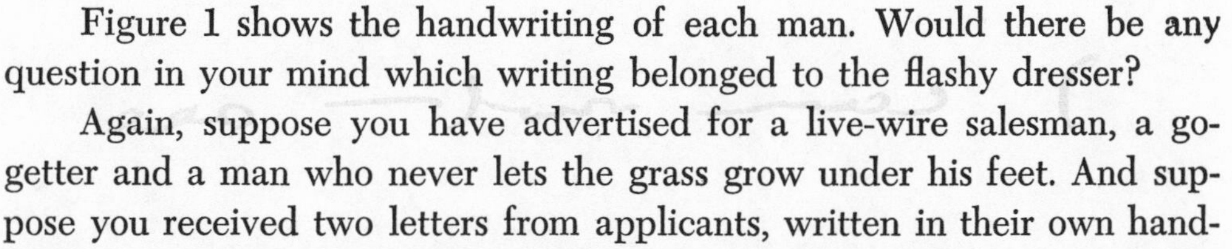

A
B

FIGURE 2

Surely you can see that the slow, over-carefully formed letters in specimen A could never have been written by an energetic hustler. It takes time to form these letters so carefully, and anyone who can waste that much time is not apt to be "on his toes" and alert. And isn't it equally obvious that the writer of specimen B cannot possibly be lazy or indolent? How could a lazy person write such an energetic script? People's characters don't change the minute they take hold of a fountain pen.

This is just pure common sense. A little reflection will convince you that the fundamental qualities in one's make-up appear unconsciously in everything he does, whether it is in sharpening a pencil, in hanging up his hat and coat, in walking, or manner of dress. Our friend, the flashy dresser, is always subconsciously determined to attract the attention of others, or he would not dress in the manner in which he does. For this reason, also, he writes with a flourish, shading his writing, making it "beautiful," and crying out, "Look at me! Here I am!"

Here is another example which requires little explanation:

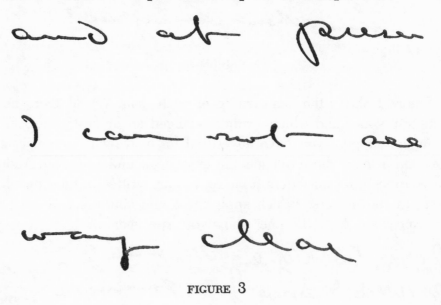

FIGURE 3

The writer could have written fully ten times as many words as he did in the space that he used. He could have written smaller and left much less space between his lines as well as words. But he did not.

He just did not seem to care how much paper he used. He is obviously an extravagant, wasteful person. If you doubt this, picture an extremely thrifty person wasting so much paper and you will readily agree that this would be entirely contrary to his make-up.

Still another example, perhaps the most obvious of all. A quick glance at the writing is all that is necessary to convince you that there is something abnormal about the person who wrote this specimen.

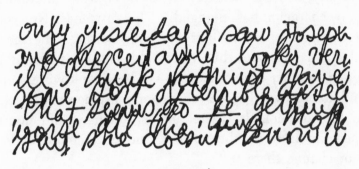

FIGURE 4

It is just as though this person's thoughts were stretched out on the paper before you—one thought running into the other, confused, mixed-up, muddled. The normal mind as a rule thinks clearly, and nobody whose thinking is normal could possibly write this tangled conglomeration of confused words.

There are thousands of other points, some more obvious and some more subtle, than those given here. There are reasons for all—concrete, definite, scientific reasons, and just as there are no two characters in the world alike, so there are no two handwritings alike.

It must be obvious, from these examples, that at least the general characteristics of a person are clearly indicated by an analysis of his handwriting. Yet in spite of this conclusion of common sense, there will be many doubting Thomases who are skeptical and who will look upon it as simply another form of fortunetelling or crystal gazing. Such people obviously know nothing about the subject.

In the first place, let it be definitely understood that handwriting analysis makes no pretense at foretelling the future, nor does it reveal the past. It is the result of years of intensive research in psychology and psychoanalysis. There are more than three hundred volumes on graphology in the New York Public Library, most of which are scientific and highly technical treatises and many are in foreign languages, written by psychologists of international reputation.

Nearly every skeptical person has asked: "How can you tell me what my character is when I don't write twice alike? On one day my writing will look one way, and the next day it will be entirely different. Does that mean that my character has changed?" The answer is: No, your character has not changed at all; neither has your writing. The inexperienced eye of the layman will cause him to think, because his writing slopes one way today and another way tomorrow—or because it will go uphill today and downhill tomorrow—that his character must necessarily change that quickly. To the graphologist there are certain hard and fast characteristics stamped indelibly on the writing, and no amount of disguise can erase them or change them.

If your writing slopes backward today, forward tomorrow, it merely reflects a mood that you are in for the time being, just as does the up- or downhill writing. If you are gloomy on Tuesday, your writing may not slope in its usual manner, and you are apt to find that it is an entirely different slope from your more natural condition of Monday. Sometimes there are two slopes in the same letter or specimen, which is an obvious indication of change of mood.

If the specimens of Monday and Tuesday were compared and studied closely, it is safe to say that the maze of minute signs (like *i* dots, *t* crosses, open *a*'s and *o*'s, shape of letters, etc.) would remain unchanged.

The very fact, indeed, that handwriting does clearly show change of mood is a proof of its validity.

Here is another objection, which shows little thought: "How can handwriting show our character when so many have learned to write in the same way?" The answer is obvious: The very fact that so many of us do learn from the same source and that no two handwritings in the world are alike, proves that our individuality is determined to show, in spite of the fact that nearly all handwritings have a common starting point. It may be added that one of the indications of an undeveloped and negative personality, in an adult, is that he writes the copybook style;

in other words, there is clearly not enough individuality in him to have caused a change from the conventional handwriting which he was taught.

A third objection, often heard, relates to thick and thin writing. "You say that thickness has a definite meaning in your analysis. But doesn't that depend upon the kind of pen point? If you use a stub pen your writing is bound to be thick." The answer is: Do you *always* use a stub pen? If you do, it is because your tendency is to write thick. If you write with a fine pen, it is because you prefer to write thin. You feel, unconsciously, that that type of writing represents you. You select the pen you habitually use, and you select it according to your manner of writing. If a writer, accustomed to using a very fine pen, writes with a stub pen for his analysis, he will not be giving a true specimen of his handwriting.

A fourth objection is, as some people have contended, that writing is purely a muscular operation, inasmuch as it is controlled by the fingers and arm. They argue that, being a muscular action, it can have no connection at all with personality. The answer to this is: Try to write a sentence while you are reading a book and see how far you get. Unlike walking or eating, during which one can read a newspaper or a book with ease, writing requires so much attention that while writing it is not possible to concentrate on anything else.

Furthermore, handwriting clearly changes with moods—such as despondency, ill health, fatigue, optimism, or elation. This is conclusive evidence that mental states have a close connection with handwriting, just as they have with many other muscular operations.

A fifth objection is: "If handwriting shows character or ability, why don't all musicians write the same, or all doctors, or all artists? Why, for instance, is the signature of Menuhin so different from that of Heifitz, while both writers are violinists?" The answer is obvious.

Musicians are not like so many automatons—turned out in a mold by the thousands. They are human beings with characteristics which differ as much as yours or mine, and consequently their writings will differ. It is true that the writing of all of them on close analysis shows some common traits, but these similarities are dominated by a multiplicity of other characteristics in which they differ widely.

Here is another very common objection: "Handwriting cannot reflect character because it can be easily disguised." The answer to this is that it is not true. It is not possible to disguise handwriting completely, because of the hundreds of tiny signs hidden in it. Observe, for example, Figures 5 and 6:

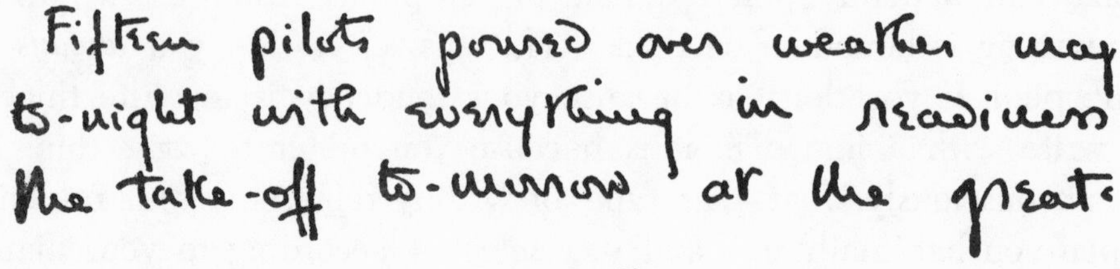

FIGURE 5

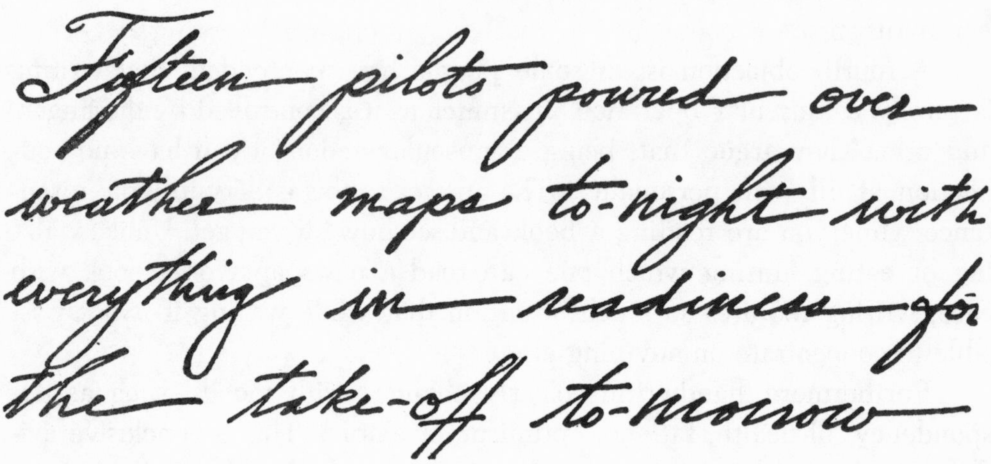

FIGURE 6

Figure 5 is a person's natural writing; Figure 6 is his attempted disguise. On the surface these writings appear totally different, but this is by no means the case. On the contrary, they are very much alike. If you compare the two words "with" in each sample you will see that they are very much alike, with the exception of the slope. The dots are all directly over the *i*'s in both samples—a point which the writer forgot to change in his second specimen. The word "off" in "take-off" is almost exactly the same in both, with the exception of the slope.

If the disguised writing were put through this book, fully seventy-five per cent of the characteristics that appear in the first specimen would be revealed in it. Note also the way the "th" is made in "everything" in the first specimen, and in "with" in the second.

While this is a clever disguise—far better than the average layman could do—it can be readily seen that there are enough points in common to convict the writer of attempting to disguise his handwriting, provided both specimens were shown. Even if only one were shown and an analysis made, most of the telltale characteristics would remain. In writing the second specimen, our friend cleverly changed the slope, the finals, the connections, and many other things, but failed to change the seemingly trivial things enumerated. Time and again people have tried to disguise their writing, but it is immediately apparent to the eye of the graphologist.

There are, however, many signs in handwriting which seem to have no common-sense connection with the character of the writer. To take a few examples: What reasoning leads graphologists to conclude that athletes make their *g's* and *p's* very long, or that people who make stencil letters are hypocritical? What right have they to say that writers of thick, muddy writing are highly sensual, or that those whose writing is very small are intellectually superior? These are bold statements and the evidence seems quite obscure. What scientific basis is there for such conclusions?

Frankly, we don't know, completely, why these peculiar signs should denote the characteristics that they do. We only know that from experience that they have been proved to be reliable, accurate, and dependable; and unquestionably there are deep psychological reasons, difficult to trace with certainty, for these more minute indications of the correspondence between handwriting and personality. When the graphologist labels certain signs with definite characteristics, he is merely making use of the results of hundreds of years of research, though he may not always know why the results occur. In this way he resembles the electrical engineer who works out and uses elaborate mathematical formulae, as well as the results of years of research in electronics, without knowing the exact nature of the atom's nucleus.

In fact, patient cataloguing and observation have taken graphology completely out of the guesswork stage and made it a deductive as well as an inductive science. Is it not logical to assume that, if, out of one thousand straightforward and reliable men, ninety-nine per cent write with straight base lines, that straight base lines indicate straightforwardness and reliability? From a mathematical standpoint, the chances of an unreliable person exhibiting this trait are extremely remote.

Graphology, in addition to being a logical interpretation of character on paper, is founded on tireless research, keen observation, and patient "cataloguing," just like most of the sciences. It is most comparable with a more or less uncertain body of knowledge, like medicine, which is not and never can be an exact science, but which is based largely on observation and research. It is founded upon the science of psychology and psychoanalysis and, though still in its infancy, it is of great practical value in hundreds of large business houses and employment agencies.

This book is based entirely upon the discoveries of graphology, and is designed primarily as an entertaining pastime. It will also prove useful as a means to better understanding among friends and acquaintances; but while it is unique in its form, it will be of great value if used according to the given directions, and can be used, therefore, in the office, as well as in the home.

HOW TO
USE THIS BOOK

Read These Directions Carefully

IN THIS BOOK the author has attempted to take the "ology" out of graphology and place the whole subject entirely in the hands of the layman. He wants particularly those people who have not the slightest knowledge of the subject to analyze handwriting. He has tried to construct this book in such a manner that anyone anywhere can take a sample of handwriting, "run it through" the lettered pages from "A" through "Q", tabulate his findings, look up meanings, and thus obtain an accurate analysis without knowing anything about graphology, either before or after. In this way all of the necessary study and tedious work is eliminated without losing any of the fascination.

The book is divided into two parts. The first consists of a number of diagrams on translucent paper. The specimen of handwriting to be analyzed is placed under each of these diagrams in turn. The number of the particular diagram that matches the specimen should be noted in each case. Letters and numbers are jotted down but no analysis is attempted.

The second part of the book consists of a complete list of the meanings of all the diagrams, as well as combinations of them.

One simply looks up the numbers, which he has recorded from the first part of the book, in order to get the analysis of the handwriting in the second part of the book.

Before making an analysis, however, it is well to bear in mind the following ten extremely important points:

1. Be sure that your conclusion is correct, before you tabulate it. A characteristic is not present to any degree unless the sign is clearly shown, and the clearer the indication of that sign and the more it is repeated, the greater will be the certainty of that characteristic being present. When a sign is displayed continually, you are safe in putting it down as a definite characteristic; the occasional signs signify minor

traits. Furthermore, your specimen may show many different forms of the *t* cross, or many different styles of *d's* or *p's*. In such cases the style appearing the most frequently indicates a dominant characteristic, and the others "occasional traits."

2. It is important that the specimen of handwriting you are testing is the *natural script* of the writer. For this reason it is best to take the last page of a letter rather than the first. Never read from post cards or diaries. If the person whose writing you are about to analyze is present, he should use the type of pen he is most accustomed to using. He should also write anything that comes into his head without being at all conscious of *what* or *how* he is writing. If the writing is not natural, the analysis will be inaccurate.

3. Many of the people have asked for the bad points as well as the good. This book lists both, and makes no attempt to flatter the reader. A number of cases will undoubtedly come up in which the undesirable traits will appear. If you find any of them in your own writing or that of a friend, don't jump to conclusions but go over your tabulations carefully, in order to make sure you have made no mistake in taking them down.

4. There are two characteristics which sweep aside all other signs. The first is the infallible sign of hypocrisy: *a's* and *o's* which are broken *at the base* (Figure 7). It is possible that writing showing this characteristic will also have a straight base line, which signifies straightforwardness and dependability. Obviously this is a contradiction. The fact, however, that this writing is so rare and the trait is so marked when it does appear, completely overshadows and eliminates the much more common sign of the even base line. No food is more healthful or beneficial than milk, but a couple of drops of potassium cyanide in a glass of milk will render it poisonous. In the same way, handwriting that may appear to be honest, reliable and straightforward can be "poisoned" by the appearance of stencil letters.

The other characteristic is muddy, feather-edge, uneven pressure writing (Figure 8) which reveals voluptuousness. This sign is much more difficult to recognize than the hypocritical writing, because a bad pen sometimes is apt to produce a similar effect. If it is certain that the pen is not to blame, you may be sure the writer is all this book says he is,

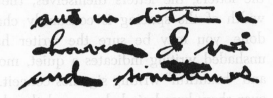

please be sure to get me that

FIGURE 7   FIGURE 8

and no favorable sign can alter the fact, for all other qualities are swallowed in this muddy tangle, which clearly is the outstanding characteristic.

5. In other cases, where two traits seem to contradict one another (which will be rare), find their relative strength by noting the one which appears the more frequently, and list it.

6. Some handwriting displays little character for the reason that the personality of the writer is not strong. In such cases, do not try to get more out of the specimen than is actually in it. If it is the conventional style, you may be sure that there is little need to look up your numbers, because such "perfect" or "beautiful" writing is always lacking in definite characteristics. Such writers have negative personalities. This also holds true for ignorant and illiterate handwriting, which can be told at a glance by anyone.

7. The best specimens for analysis are those written in ink on unlined paper. Their length should be at least fifty words. It does not matter what is written as the context has nothing to do with the analysis.

8. The sex of a person cannot be determined by handwriting, because there are many women who possess a great many masculine characteristics, and vice versa.

9. An important thing to observe in making an analysis is the general style of the handwriting. This is not mentioned in the Key Section, but it is nevertheless significant.

When you pick up a sample of handwriting for analysis, *glance at the general style before starting to put it through this book*. If the style is hasty, it shows an energetic, spontaneous personality. If the style is slow and rounded, it indicates a lazy nature—one lacking in spontaneity and initiative. If the writing looks dirty and "uneven," if the slope of

15

the letters, the letters themselves, the thickness of the writing and the width of the spacing is constantly changing and the writing is slowly done, you may be sure the writer has a shady character. Very thin, unshaded writing indicates a quiet, modest person, just as ornate, shaded and "beautiful" writing signifies conceit. Corrected words and words done over show broadmindedness and the desire and willingness to see one's own faults. Careful punctuation means attention to details and shows a meticulous person, while careless punctuation means the opposite. Too much punctuation and unnecessary underscoring signify sentimentality. Backhand writing nearly always shows self-consciousness, hidden emotions and many inhibitions—particularly if it is thick writing. Take these facts into consideration before you start your analysis.

10. A final word about combinations. A number of these combinations are given in the second part of this book, but we have hardly scratched the surface of all the possibilities. There are, of course, many millions just as there are many millions of characters, and it is obviously impossible to list all of them. As you become better acquainted with the use of this book, you will be able to make up your own combinations in addition to those given here. You will know from experience that the danger combination A-2, K-1 and M-4 is more likely to overshadow the C-5 or C-6 slope which is fine characterization. You will be able to add an L number or a Q number to one or more of your regular combinations and find new character readings that are not in this book. The more you use the book and the more familiar you become with the styles and their combinations, the more vast will be the number of combinations you can make up for yourself and hence, the more valuable the book. Don't try making up your own combinations in the beginning, just use those given here.

The Handwriting Analyzer is extremely simple to use. Just follow the directions at the top of each diagram sheet and mark down what you find without thinking of what it means. After you have gone through each of these sheets and have a complete listing of letter-numbers, then turn to the analysis key section on Page 55 and find out what these letter-numbers mean. Remember to look for *combinations* as well as the individual letter-numbers. If you follow these simple rules, your analysis will be more than eighty-five per cent correct.

A
SAMPLE
ANALYSIS

WHENEVER possible it is always a good idea, before you start, to know whether the writer of the specimen of handwriting you are about to analyze is a man or a girl and whether he or she is young, middle aged or old. It is also important to make sure that the writing is the natural writing of the person and not done "specially for the occasion." If it is done on the spot it must be written without being self-conscious—just as though the writer were taking lecture notes in ink on unlined paper. Now let us examine the sample given here for analysis.

This is the beginning of a letter from a middle-aged married woman, and it is obvious, from the first impression, that she is modest and very unassuming since the script is neat and definitely unpretentious. The words fairly drip off the pen and the spacing of the lines is wide and even. Everything is clear and clean about this writing, and you get a feeling of calmness, smoothness and perfect ease as you read it.

Starting on page 25, the A page of the comparison diagrams, and following the directions on that page, we see how remarkably straight the base lines are and how well they stay on the line A-B. We therefore put down A-1 and go to the next page.

Following the directions on the B page we see that there is a slight slope to the lines and they come into the space 1 which, on the B page, is B-1. We add this to our A notation thus: A-1, B-1. Then we go to the C page.

Following the directions on the C page we see that the slope of the letters is vertical and fits into the diagram 1. This is the C page, so we write C-1 after our A-1 and B-1.

Continuing this procedure through all the other pages, we have the following list of notations:

A-1, B-1, C-1, D-2, E-3, F-1, G-2 and G-4, H-2, J-2, K-2, L-2 and L-3, M-2, N-1, and P-2.

Now, examining the letters separately and comparing them with the samples on the Q page, we see that the small *h*'s and *d*'s are similar to those shown in Q-4 (note the *h* in "have" and the *d* in "doubt"). We also see that the lower loop letters *g* and *y* are gentle and round as shown in Q-24. The *i* dots are high and to the right as shown in Q-28 and

Q-29. Nearly all of the *t* crosses are very short like those shown in Q-42, Q-43 and Q-44. Other Q numbers will be seen to be Q-50, Q-51, Q-73 and Q-76. Add these Q notations to your list and we are ready for the analysis.

Turning to the analysis section on page 57 we see from the A page that A-1 is straightforward and dependable. Looking at the combinations we see that we have K-2 and M-2 on our list; hence the writer is honest, sincere and truthful. Since there are no other combinations that fit our list we turn to the B page. B-1 gives us a healthy ambition and a generally optimistic nature, a person who is hard to discourage. There is no combination on this page that fits our list, so we go to the C page.

Dear Jerome.

We are so glad that you and Dorothy could spend the Xmas Holidays with us and enjoy seeing Judy Ann.

She certainly is, without doubt the most attractive baby I have ever seen and we are all very proud of her.

We expect to spend New Years Eve at the Siegels in Pound Ridge and are so sorry that you can't join us.

C-3 shows that the writer has head control over emotions. She has a fine analytical mind with good reasoning powers and keen judgment. She could be a creative writer.

The D-2 size is very small but not in the class with the D-1. It shows, nevertheless, an excellent mental equipment, good sound judgment, and a highly developed critical sense. The E-3 notation tells us the writer could be a good organizer and executive. She is a good judge of character and has a fine sense of justice. The spacing is even, so we have a person with firmly rooted ideas and very strong convictions who is interested in cultural subjects. The F-1 notation shows that the writer has both feet on the ground and is quite practical.

G-4 shows what is known as the "garland." Note the round connections at the base in words like "and," "have," "ever," and "with." These are good examples of G-4 which, according to the analysis given, is a writer who is adaptable, receptive and responsive. A person who is peace-loving and good natured, avoiding all loud arguments and fights. She is not a hustler and is inclined to take the line of least resistance most of the time.

H-2 shows spirituality and refinement. Quiet, modest tastes and a simple, unassuming, and unaffected personality. Never tries to make an impression and is sometimes a bit timid and bashful. Kindness is also evident in this H-2 script.

J-2 is the average in this form and means nothing special by itself.

K-2 shows a painstaking and conscientious nature and here again we see the A-1, M-2 combination.

L-2 supports the H-2 notation. She hates to be conspicuous and hardly ever "holds forth" in a group.

In L-3 the long finals in "and" in the first line, "seen" in the fifth line, and "and" in the next to the last line do not contradict the short finals found elsewhere, and we have a person who is generous and considerate.

M-2 again supports the sincerity and truthfulness combination A-1, K-2 and M-2.

N-1 shows a practical and logical nature who is somewhat argumentative. Difficult to sway from her opinions.

The P-2 notation is clear. The capitals are low but not too low. Here again we have simplicity of taste and modesty.

By looking up the Q numbers on the list, Q-4, 24, 28, 29, 42, 43, 44, 50, 51, 73, 74 and 76, we can fill out the rest of the analysis which, when summed up and written out, turns out to be the following:

The writer is a thoroughly sincere, truthful and dependable person who, by virtue of circumstances did not make the most of her excellent mental equipment. She is evidently too unassuming and modest and lacks the necessary push and incentive to have a successful career. Knowing from the start that she is a middle-aged married woman, it may be taken for granted that she has devoted her talents to creating a happy home for her husband and her children. Just as everything about the script is clean and clear and calm, so it is with the writer. Her simplicity and lack of pretension coupled with her generosity and her giving of herself have undoubtedly been responsible to a great degree for the happiness of her married life and have won her many loyal friends. She is adaptable, receptive, responsive and peace loving but lacks a definite initiative and ability to "blow her own trumpet." She is kind and considerate, with a fine mentality and aesthetic sense. This, together with a good sense of humor, makes her very popular and wins many loyal friends. With all this to her credit one would naturally think she would be a J-3 writer, but this is not the case. She likes people, but she is not too good a mixer—only because of her aversion to being conspicuous and pushing herself. She is practical and logical and the formation of the capital *I* in the fifth line shows a fine healthy self-respect without a trace of conceit.

COMPARISON
DIAGRAMS

Can You Stay on a Straight Line?

PLACE the specimen of the handwriting to to be analyzed underneath this sheet so that the bottom of any one of the written lines rests on line AB. Note carefully whether the writing stays on the line or whether it bobs continuously up and down, above and below the line. If it stays on A-B put down A-1, otherwise put down A-2. Make sure that if the writing bobs up and down it does so continuously before putting it down as A-2. Occasional unevenness means nothing special.

A ——————————————————————————————— B

Does Your Writing Run Up- or Downhill?

Place the specimen of handwriting underneath this sheet so that the edge of the paper on which the writing appears comes along the vertical line AB, starting one particular line of writing at C. Note within which space this writing rests and record it under your A number, thus: A-1
B-3

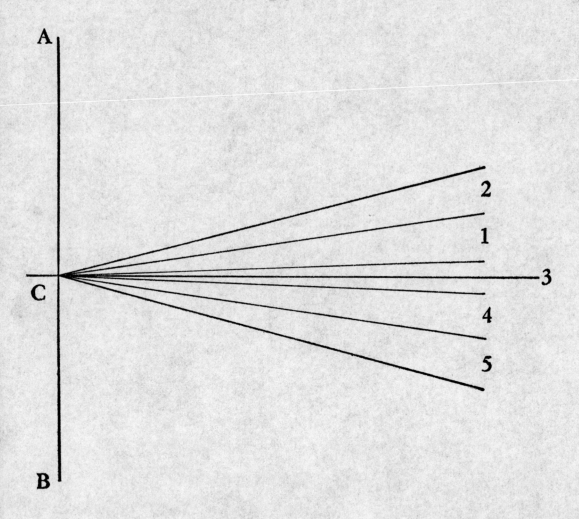

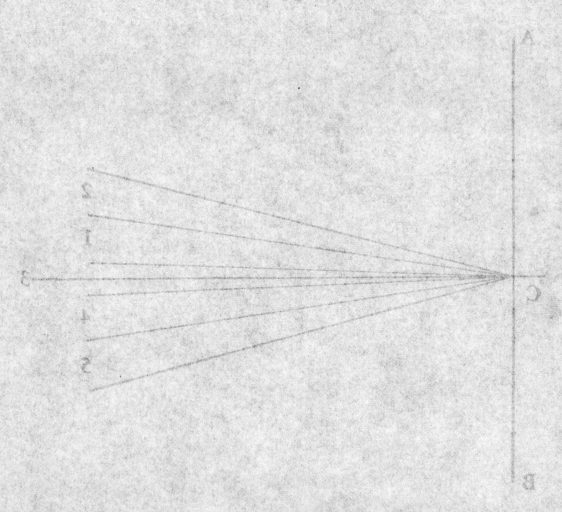

B

Does Your Writing Run Up- or Downhill?

Place the specimen of handwriting underneath this sheet so that the edge of the paper on which the writing appears comes along the vertical line AB, starting one particular line of writing at C. Note within which space this writing rests and record it under your A number, thus: A-1.

B-5

Which Way Does Your Handwriting Slope?

Place the specimen underneath this sheet so that the tall letters like *b, d, h,* and *l* fit the slope of one of the eight slope diagrams given below. Put the number of your slope below the B number.

Two slopes in the same writing indicates moodiness.

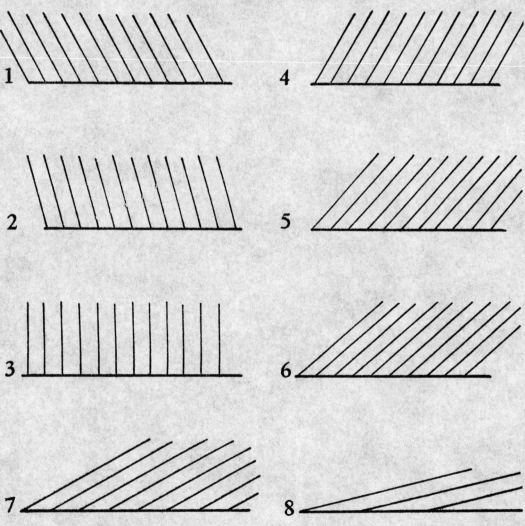

Which Way Does Your Handwriting Slope?

Place the specimen underneath this sheet so that the tall letters like b, d, h, and l fit the slope of one of the eight slope diagrams given below. Put the number of your slope below the it number.

Two slopes in the same writing indicate moodiness.

How Large Are Your Small Letters?

Fit the small letters of your specimen in between the correct pair of parallel lines and note the number below your C number.

1

2

3

4

5

6

7

How Much Space Is Between Your Lines?

The amount of space between the lines in a page of handwriting is considered here. Look at your specimen and determine about how far apart the lines of writing are compared with those shown below.

1 *before have we seen many a / this kind of handwriting / shows a mind that is some / disorderly for nobody whose / mind is good and clear w / write like this.*

2 *This is the average spacin / of handwriting. maybe the _ / loop letter will touch the b / below but it wont matter / the spacing is more or le*

3 *Spacing as wide apart a / shows a neat and orderly / and is also an indicatio / extravagant nature. So*

How Much Space Is Between Your Lines?

The amount of space between the lines in a page of handwriting is considered here. Look at your specimen and determine about how far apart the lines of writing are compared with those shown below.

How Wide Are Your Left Margins?

This page concerns margins—narrow or wide. It shows five different margin widths, the line AB representing the edge of the paper and the left edge of the boxes representing the left edge of the handwriting. Compare the width of the margin on your specimen with the width of the margins shown and note the key number closest to it. A very narrow margin is given in F-1; an exceptionally wide one in F-5.

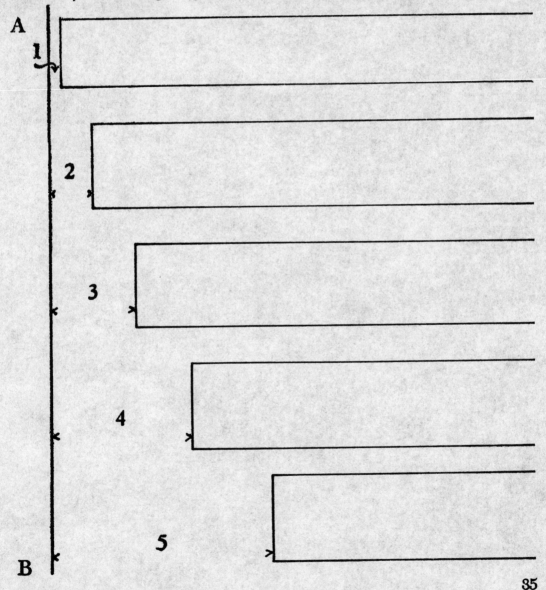

How Wide Are Your Left Margins?

This page concerns margins—narrow or wide. It shows five different margin widths, the line AB representing the edge of the paper and the left edge of the box representing the left edge of the handwriting. Compare the width of the margin on your specimen with the width of the margins shown and note the key number closest to it. A very narrow margin is given in F-1; an exceptionally wide one in F-5.

Are Your Letters Rounded or Pointed? Garlands and Arcades.

This page gives examples of pointed and rounded tops on small *m's* and *n's*. It also shows gracefully rounded connections at the base otherwise known as GARLANDS and gracefully arched tops of *m's* and *n's* otherwise known as ARCADES. Look at the tops and bases of the letters and compare them with the specimens shown here. Don't confuse G-5 with G-3.

1 *inning in*   Always pointed or nearly so

2 *inning in*   Sometimes pointed

3 *inning in*   Never pointed

Bottoms of
letter connections curved

4 *inning in*    GARLAND

Curved at tops

5 *inning in*   ARCADE

37

Are Your Letters Rounded or Pointed?
Garlands and Arcade.

This page gives examples of pointed and rounded tops on small m's and n's. It also shows gracefully rounded connections at the base otherwise known as GARLANDS and gracefully arched tops of m's and n's otherwise known as ARCADES. Look at the tops and bases of the letters and compare them with the specimens shown here. Don't confuse G-S with G-B.

How Thick Are Your Letters?

The thickness of the letters is considered here. If the writing is very thin, it is H-1; if it is very thick and heavy, it will match H-5 or H-6, as the case may be. Note that the H-3 is divided into three parts: writing that is evenly thick throughout, writing that is naturally shaded (down strokes heavier than the up strokes), and writing that is shaded for effect. If the letters are all evenly thick, put it down as H-3A; if shaded naturally, it is H-3B; and if shaded for effect, it is H-3C. Before deciding on H-7, which shows uneven, smeary and dirty writing, make sure that a bad pen has nothing to do with it and that it is the natural writing of the subject.

1 *this very thin writ is an indication*

2 *fine writing writ like this shows*

3A *this is about the average in*

3B *is writing is shaa turally and sho*

3C *Mrs P. Monaha*

4 *writing like th shows a chara*

5 *Of course the pen will have a lot*

6 *this writing si a great deal*

7 *Mr Solomon as y— and in lott— lovin & vri and sommtim s*

Are Your Letters Compressed or Extended?

On this sheet you will see boxes to measure extended and compressed writing. These boxes fit small, medium, large, or very large scripts. The first column, J-1, indicates compressed writing; the second column average writing, and the third extended writing.

First determine about how large the writing is by fitting the small letters *a*, *c*, *m*, etc., between the top and bottom of the box and consider in which row you will test it. Then choose a six-letter word and find out into which box it will fit.

1   **2**   **3**

Small writing

Medium writing

Large writing

Very large writing

41

Are Your Letters Compressed or Extended?

On this sheet you will see boxes to measure extended and compressed writing. These boxes fit small, medium, large or very large scripts. The first column, 1-1, indicates compressed writing, the second column average writing, and the third extended writing.

First determine about how large the writing is by fitting the small letters a, c, m, etc. between the top and bottom of the box and consider in which row you will fall. Then choose a six-letter word and find out into which box it will fit.

1   2   3

Small writing

Medium writing

Large writing

Very large writing

K

Are Your Letters All Even in Size?

Even and uneven small letters play an important part in analysis. This page shows four different samples. If the small letters in your specimen vary in size continually—if, in other words, the small letters are sometimes large and sometimes small and this characteristic is noticeable throughout the entire handwriting, write down K-1. If all the small letters are *about* the same size (they will seldom be exactly the same size) write down K-2. The other two diagrams are self-explanatory.

1 *Small letters constantly varying in size like this writing*

2 *Small letters all even or nearly even like this writing*

3 *Small letters tapering like this*

4

Are Your Letters All Even in Size?

Even and uneven small letters play an important part in analysis. This page shows four different samples. If the small letters in your specimen vary in size continually—in other words, the small letters are sometimes large and sometimes small and this characteristic is noticeable throughout the entire handwriting, write down K-1. If all the small letters are about the same size (they will seldom be exactly the same size) write down K-2. The other two diagrams are self-explanatory.

1. *Small letters constantly varying in size like this writing*

2. *Small letters all even or nearly even like this writing*

3. *Small letters tapering like this*

4.

Compare Your Finals with These

Examine the finals on words ending in *e, h, m, n, r, s,* and *t;* compare the length and nature of these finals with the twenty-two examples shown below. This should be done with great care in order to get an accurate analysis. You will probably have more than one listing from this page.

1 *name* ←- Finals absent

2 *name* ← Finals short

3 *name* ← Finals long

4 *name* ← Finals very long

5 *name* ← Finals rise vertically

6 *name* ← Finals curl over

7 *name* ← Finals ascend to right

8 *name* ← Finals curl under

9 *name* ← Finals weak and descend to right

10 *name* ← Finals strong and descend to right

11 *name* ← Finals descend vertically

12 *name* ← Fish hook turned up

13 *name* ← Fish hook turned down

14 *name* ← Finals short and curved

15 *name* ← Finals thick and clublike

16 *name* ← Finals thick and snakelike

17 *name* ← Finals long and curved

18 *name* ← Finals used to fill what would otherwise be blank spaces

19 *name* ← Finals lasso-like

20 *name* ← Finals turned down

21 *name* ← Finals curl like pigtails

22 *name*

M

Do You Open Your *a's* and *o's*?

This page is concerned with the small letters *a* and *o*. Look carefully at your specimen and note the *tops of these letters*. Are the *a's* and *o's* open at the top as shown in M-1? Are they sometimes closed at the top as shown in M-2? Or are they always closed at the top as shown in M-3? It is up to you to decide.

If the tops of the *a's* and *o's* are tightly knotted, write down M-4. *If the bottoms* of the *a's* and *o's* are open, write down M-5.

1 *a and o open at top like this*

2 *a and o sometimes closed at top like this*

3 *a and o always closed at top like this*

4 *a and o tightly knotted at top like this - also s at bottom*

5 *a and o open at bottom like this*

Are Your Letters Connected?

Here we see connected and disconnected letters. Compare your specimen with those on this page. If the letters are all, or nearly all connected, write down N-1; if they are nearly all disconnected, write down N-2; and if they are all disconnected, write down N-3. If many of the words are connected. write down N-4.

1 *Letters nearly always connected like this.*

2 *Letters nearly always disconnected like this.*

3 *Letters always disconnected like This.*

4 *Words connected like this*

P

How High Are Your Capital Letters?

Compare the height of your capitals with those shown on this page and add the number of the corresponding size to your list.

When capitals are neither high nor low it means nothing special.

1 *Mr. and Mrs John Endicott, new york city*

These capitals are very low

2 *Mr and Mrs. John Endicott New York city*

These capitals are low

3 *Mr. and Mrs. John Endicott New York City*

These capitals are high

4 *Mr. and Mrs. John Endicott New York City*

These capitals are very high

Compare Your Small Letters with These

The following examples are different forms of a few of the important letters

1 ℓ ℓ ℓ ℳ ℳ The initial stroke begins at right and swings left forming a loop

2 ℓ ℓ Initial downstroke made without loop

3 ℓ ℓ ℳ ℎ 𝑝 Initial hook instead of loop

4 b h p h Made like small printed letters

5 d Stem high by comparison with other letters

6 d Stem low by comparison with other letters

7 δ δ δ Curved upward and projecting to the right

8 ∂ ∂ ∂ ∂ ∂ℓ Curved upward and back (Greek D)

9 d d ⊕ ⊕ Made with wide loop

10 d d Upstroke separated from the downstroke and does not cross it

11 δ δ Curved upward ending in a spiral curve

12 q ℎ ℎ Final stroke descends below the line

13 ∂ ℓ 𝓌 Lasso loops on letters

14 ℓ ℓ ℓ Not looped, return stroke to right

Q

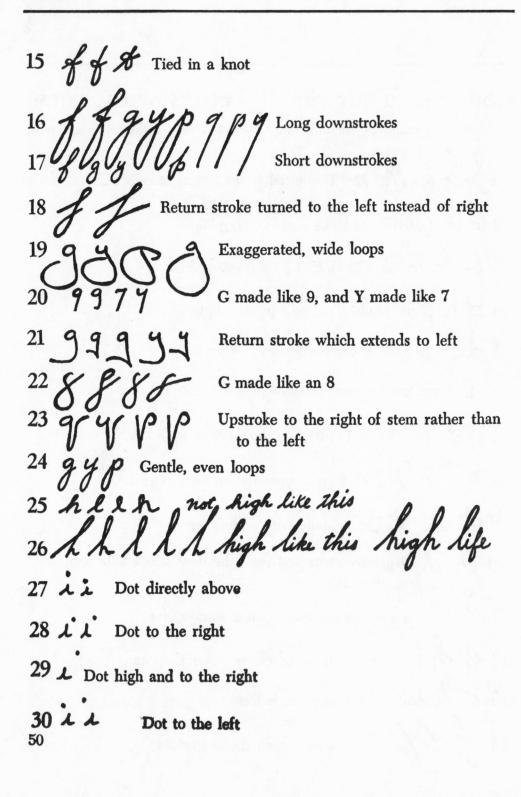

15   Tied in a knot

16   Long downstrokes

17   Short downstrokes

18   Return stroke turned to the left instead of right

19   Exaggerated, wide loops

20   G made like 9, and Y made like 7

21   Return stroke which extends to left

22   G made like an 8

23   Upstroke to the right of stem rather than to the left

24   Gentle, even loops

25   not high like this

26   high like this   high life

27   Dot directly above

28   Dot to the right

29   Dot high and to the right

30   Dot to the left

31 *i*   Dot low and directly over

32 *i*   Dot heavy and thick

33 *i*   Dot light and weak

34 *i*   Dot in the form of a circle

35 *i i i i i*   Dots elongated like dashes

36 *i i i i i*   Dots like commas or arrowheads

37 *i*   Dot omitted

38 *w* and *n* like *w* and *u*

39 *m* and *n* unlike *w* and *u*

40 *r r r r r r r*

41 *n n*   Rounded at top

42 *t t*   Short crosses

43 *t t*   Crosses to right

44 *t t t*   Crosses to left

45 *t t*   Long crosses

46 *t*   Long cross to right

47 *t*   Thin cross

Q

48   *Thick cross*

49   *Weak cross*

50   Cross very low

51   Cross very high

52   Cross eliminated

53   Cross slanting slightly up

54   Cross slanting slightly down

55   Cross slanting decidedly down

56   Cross slanting decidedly down and curved

57   With hook up at end

58   With hook down at end

59   Cross with hook at left

60   Cross turned down at right not hooked

61   Cross curved or scroll shaped

62   Cross beginning thin and growing thick

63   Cross beginning thick and growing thin

64   **Unusually heavy cross**

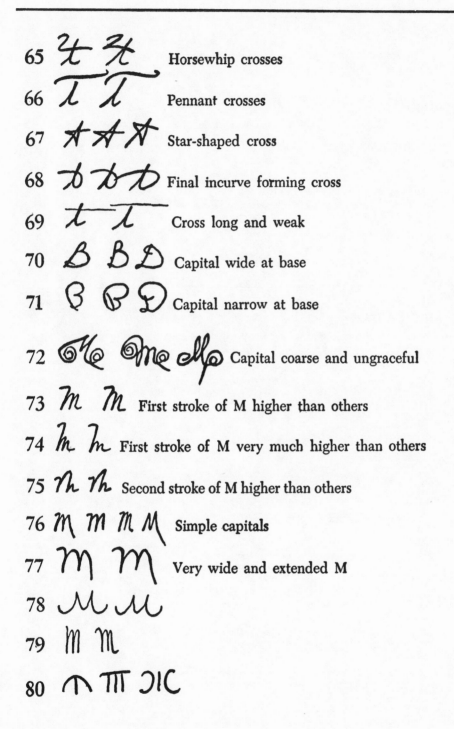

65 Horsewhip crosses

66 Pennant crosses

67 Star-shaped cross

68 Final incurve forming cross

69 Cross long and weak

70 Capital wide at base

71 Capital narrow at base

72 Capital coarse and ungraceful

73 First stroke of M higher than others

74 First stroke of M very much higher than others

75 Second stroke of M higher than others

76 Simple capitals

77 Very wide and extended M

78

79

80

KEY SECTION

THE CHARACTERISTICS ANALYZED

In each bracketed combination *all* the numbers must be present for undesirable characteristics. In all other cases, the greater the percentage of numbers present, the stronger the tendency toward the trait mentioned.

The Base Line

A-1   This has to do with the base line of the handwriting, regardless of whether it slopes uphill or downhill. If the base line is straight or nearly so . . . if it stays on the line A-B or even if it goes above it or below it occasionally, the writer is straightforward and dependable (provided M-5 or H-7 are not present). This A-1 writing will be found in most specimens because, fortunately, most people are straightforward and dependable; but if it isn't, this does not mean that the writer is deceitful or dishonest. It merely says that the writer is apt to be careless about small things. Only in combination with other traits will A-2 show undesirable characteristics.

In combination with:

C-4 or C-5 D-5 or D-6 J-3 and Q-7	A good entertainer and a lot of fun plus a bit of a flirt.
K-2	Honesty.
K-2 M-1 or M-2	Sincerity and truthfulness.
K-2 M-3	Loyalty, sincerity and secretiveness. He can keep a secret beautifully.
C-5 or C-6 D-5 or D-6 K-2 M-1	Much too frank and outspoken. Lacking in tact and discretion.
C-4 H-3C	Too conventional to have any definite personality. General lack of ambition.

A-1 in combination with:

D-5 or D-6
H-4 or H-5
Q-39 or Q-23
P-4
} This fellow is not easy to get along with. He is brusque and self-assertive and wants his own way all the time.

C-3
D-1
} Here is a real SOMEBODY or VIP. A writer, scholar or professor with excellent mental equipment, culture, critical ability and judgment.

C-6
G-3
H-3B
} A somewhat dull person who is generally lacking in humor and a little slow to catch on to things. A "good soul," but a bit of a bore.

E-2 (uneven)
H-5
Q-3
Q-23
} You may be sure this writer will always give you a long argument.

D-6
H-4
K-2
M-1 or M-2
L-7
} A very bold, outspoken and self-confident person who has great capacity for physical work and a passion for eating and material pleasures. He is honest and trustworthy but a bit difficult to get along with.

L-4 or L-7
Q-47
} A little too independent for his own good.

G-1 or G-2
D-5
Q-9
} A good talker and entertainer. Inclined to be a bit spoiled and very susceptible to flattery.

C-5 or C-6
H-2
Q-13 or Q-67
} A highly sensitive and very emotional individual.

A-2   This continual bobbing up and down above and below a straight line shows carelessness about small things. Hardly ever on time for an appointment, generally sloppy about his appearance, and not altogether reliable in small matters, yet honest and sincere. This A-2 writing, in combination with K-1 and M-4 is nearly always bad, showing deceit, dishonesty and evasiveness. Beware of this combination but be sure that it is there before you decide. Do not jump to conclusions.

In combination with:

D-2
N-3   }   Original and creative with lots of enthusiasm.
Q-8   Critical, irritable and somewhat absent-
                 minded.

B-2
D-3   }   A dreamer who overlooks details and is not
Q-51   very dependable. Somewhat impractical es-
                 pecially if F-4 is present.

K-1   Inclined to be careless in money matters.
                 Not dependable for anything requiring con-
                 stant responsibility.

K-1
M-4   }   Deceitful and dishonest.

C-3   }   Carelessness, irresponsibility, vacillation and
M-3 or M-4   a generally weak character especially if Q-49
                 is present.

G-1
K-1
L-12   }   Sly and shifty and not to be trusted.
M-4

H-7 or   }   A perfect example of what to avoid. Here is
                 a liar, a hypocrite, a vulgar and coarse indi-
M-5   vidual. Beware of this totally bad writing.

B

The Slope of the Lines

THE SLOPE OF *the lines, whether they run uphill or downhill, determines the spirit and ambition of the writer. They generally reflect a particular mood: uphill shows optimism and ambition and downhill the reverse. In many instances the downhill slope shows fatigue, exhaustion and perhaps sickness. Slopes frequently change with moods, so too much attention should not be paid to them. When the last letter or two droop downward it is an infallible sign of the blues. If the slope of lines is always the same and does not change, you may be sure of the following:*

B-1   Plenty of healthy ambition is shown here. Generally optimistic and hard to discourage.

In combination with:

G-1 or G-2 H-3 or H-4	If this is hastily written the writer is a wide awake "go-getter." A good salesman or business man generally.
Q-51	A bit of a dreamer whose head is nearly always in the clouds.
E-3 F-4 or F-5 Q-51	An impractical person who usually has wild ideas and schemes which seldom work.
H-1 Q-79	A timid soul who has high aspirations and ideals but little push or initiative.

B-2   This writer is much too buoyant for his own good. He should get down to earth and quit kidding himself. His over-optimism, restlessness and exaggerated ambition are his worst enemies.

60

B-3   Composure and self-control. This is the average slope.

In combination with:

E-3
G-1 or G-2   }   Business ability.
N-1 or N-4

H-1   }   This writer is far too timid to get anywhere.
J-1   The poor fellow is filled with fears about his
L-9   abilities and he is definitely his own worst
Q-33 or Q-49   enemy.

L-12   }   A fine sense of humor is indicated in this
Q-36 or Q-57   writing.

B-4   This poor fellow is generally at odds with the world. He is out of step with his fellow men, continually looking on the gloomy side of everything. He is oversensitive and lacks the necessary push to get ahead. Before accepting this analysis, make sure that this slope will not change tomorrow or the next day. If this B-4 slope is temporary, it shows tiredness, physical exhaustion and perhaps sickness.

In combination with:

C-6 or C-7   }   This writer usually gives way to discouragement and his morale is nearly always low. He worries and frets over little things and is hard to cheer up.

Q-35   Worry, irritability. If the last letter droops you may be sure the writer gets the blues.

B-5   Extreme grief and despondency bordering on melancholia. Perhaps this writer should see a psychiatrist.

     NOTE: Two or more different slopes in the lines of a specimen show a changeable nature, blowing hot one day and cold the next. Such a writer is moody, especially if C-6 or C-7 is present. These changeable slopes of lines in the same specimen, if combined with the A-2, K-1, M-4 combination, emphasize the bad character of the writer.

C

The Slope of Handwriting

THE AVERAGE *slope of handwriting is C-4, which is slightly to the right. Since this is the easiest way to write, being in the direction of the reading, you can say with assurance that the C-4 slope is the one of "least resistance" and is therefore the conventional slope. Such writers show a desire to comply with convention and the things dictated by convention. As the writing slopes more and more to the right the emotions of the writer become stronger and stronger until, in extreme cases like C-8, they get out of control and the writer becomes emotionally irresponsible. Just as the normal slope shows* compliance *with convention so the backhand slope shows* defiance *of convention—a resistance to doing what everyone else does, and that is why so many youngsters of college age write the backhand slope. They have rebelled "inwardly" against the "don'ts" and "you mustn't" of their early childhood. The vertical slope shows head control and a healthy self-reliance.*

C-1
or
C-2

In young people, particularly in college girls, this shows a definite self-consciousness and, in many cases, self-centeredness and selfishness. These young writers are very emotional, but at the right time and place. They seldom show their true desires and hence they are nearly always "bottled up" emotionally. They have an inward longing to be different, to defy convention and to live a sort of Bohemian life. They are loyal, sincere, trustworthy and tremendously affectionate but are difficult to know real well . . . and many of them don't even know themselves. In the college boy this slope shows a desire to break away from the parent and live "as I darn please." In middle age it shows an introvert of the first water with a strong indication of conceit.

In combination with:

D-4 or D-5
H-4 or H-5 } Cruelty.
L-15

62

C-3   A general lack of spontaneous emotion and a definite head control. An analytical mind with good reasoning powers and keen judgment. Dominance of intellect over emotions. Those who write the vertical hand usually make good creative writers.

In combination with:

D-1   What a marvelous handwriting this is. If this is your natural script you are to be congratulated, for you are a person of rare intellect, culture and imagination. Your critical sense is highly developed and you have keen judgment. This is the handwriting of scholars, scientists, philosophers, many literary people and deep thinkers. It is the infallible sign of a very high I.Q., for it is safe to say that no person of ordinary ability writes this size.

D-3
E-3   Critical ability and good sound judgment. A strong personality.
G-2

G-3   A rather good soul, but somewhat dull and bromidic. He is a bit of a bore.
H-3B

P-4   Arrogant, opinionated and self-contained.
Q-66 or Q-77

                               A bit of an actor who loves to show off. Must have attention and admiration at all times. Too spoiled for his own good. Though jolly and somewhat entertaining, this person gets a bit tiresome after a while. He is too much of an egoist to have many friends.
D-5 or D-6
H-4

C-4   Good self-control and willingness to abide by convention.

In combination with:

E-2   Business ability. A good executive with a flair for organization and system. Would make a fine efficiency expert.
G-1
N-1

C-4 in combination with:

J-3
Q-38 or Q-24 } An amiable and friendly person.

B-3
Q-44 } Hesitation and procrastination. Well meaning but ineffectual. Always busy with something or other but never ready. Slow and cautious in most undertakings.

H-1
Q-49 } No mind of his own. Easily dissuaded and influenced.

G-3
H-3B
P-4
Q-77 } An "empty barrel." If you could buy this fellow for what he is actually worth and sell him for what he thinks he is worth, you would be a millionaire. A commonplace and dull personality.

E-2
F-1 or F-2
G-1 or G-2
N-2
Q-26 } A bright and alert but somewhat conventional person with certain definite abilities along creative lines. A good copywriter or idea man. Practical and down-to-earth type with good earning capacity.

C-5
or
C-6 Generosity, sympathy and sincerity. No airs or pomp shown in this healthy slope. Affectionate, warm nature provided the danger signals M-5, H-7 and the complete combination M-4, A-2 and K-1 are not present.

In combination with:

H-2
K-2
M-1 or M-2 } A fine, sincere, warm and affectionate person who is generous, modest and unassuming. A good listener who is nearly always sympathetic and understanding. An excellent friend to have.

D-3
Q-51 } An excellent imagination which should be put to use in some sort of creative work.

A-2 H-2 K-1 L-15 or L-16 M-4	Don't be fooled by this rather innocent-looking writing. Examine it closely and see if it contains all or very nearly all of these combinations. If it does, the writer puts on a fine front, appearing to be a nice, quiet and respectable person, but he is a sly, evasive smoothie who is not to be trusted.
G-1 H-3A N-1 or N-2	Animation. Quick on the trigger mentally and physically, especially if the writing is illegible. A good salesman or sales executive.
H-1 Q-67	High strung and sensitive. Feelings easily hurt. Won't take criticism. Sincere, loyal and a bit stubborn.
N-3 Q-35 Q-46	Irritable and jumpy. Usually in a hurry to get things done. Critical and intolerant. A good sense of humor.
H-4 or H-5	This writer is apt to sulk if things aren't just to his liking. Feelings easily hurt. Susceptible to the charms of the opposite sex. Excitable, sentimental and generally lacking in self-control. Loves to eat and indulge in other physical pleasures. If Q-16 is present you may be sure this writer is an athlete.
H-1 or H-2 Q-24	Charity and altruism.

C-7 Very highly sensitive and emotional. If words are underlined and punctuation is carefully done, the writer is extremely sentimental. Very little self-control is shown in this writing.

C-8 Fortunately this writing is rare. It is almost horizontal and shows total irresponsibility. These writers are apt to be fanatic and occasionally they can be dangerous.

D

The Size of the Small Letters

IF THE *writing is very small and natural (not done to fit into small spaces as in the case of a postcard or margin of a paper) fine intelligence and powers of concentration are indicated. Such writers hardly ever care for physical comforts or showiness in dress, and they seldom give a hoot about what others think of them. They are usually creators and thinkers and the smaller the writing, the more intellectual is the writer. Large writing, on the other hand (if it is natural and not done for a message on an overlarge sheet of paper), does not show stupidity. It shows restlessness, a general lack of concentration, a desire to be noticed and praised and a love of grandeur. It also shows arrogance, poor observation, courage, generosity and enthusiasm. The average writing D-3 or D-4 means nothing particular by itself and must be judged with combinations.*

D-1   This is writing of the intellectual. No person of mediocre attainment writes this size. It is truly wonderful writing if it is natural and not done to get a great many words into a small space. It shows enormous concentration and amazing mentality. It is usually the writing of brilliant scholars, philosophers, creative writers and scientists and all others whose mental equipment is far above the average. It is nearly always vertical, showing head control, an analytical mind and keen judgment. The D-1 writer is seldom, if ever, interested in making an impression on others and has little or no concern for luxurious living and physical comforts or personal appearance in manner of dress. Einstein is a D-1 writer.

In combination with:

E-3
N-1   } Great creative ability. A leader in the field of thought; an intellectual giant who is critical and intolerant.

E-1
J-1   } This writer is stingy and petty. He is fussy and mean in spite of his fine mind.
Q-35

D-2 This writer has an excellent mind, far above the average, which can concentrate on details and grasp and size up a situation correctly. He has fine judgment, keen perception and a highly developed critical sense. The D-2 writer thinks much and says little. He is tolerant and peaceful but is generally lacking in self-confidence.

D-3
or
D-4 This is the average size of handwriting showing adaptability and a well-balanced mind (provided K-1, M-4 or M-5 and H-7 are absent).

In combination with:

E-3 F-4 G-3 Q-8	A docile, peace-loving, aesthetic and somewhat impractical nature.
N-4 Q-43	Stubborn and impatient.
C-6 H-4 L-18	Suspicion and jealousy. This writer must be handled with tact and discretion.
J-2 or J-3 M-1 or M-2 Q-9	This writer has the ability of expressing himself in clear and forcible language. He is definitely demonstrative.
G-2 or G-3 Q-31 or Q-42 Letters carefully made K-2	This writer is careful and accurate. Anything he undertakes to do will be done well.
K-4 M-4 Q-44	A cagey and crafty individual. A little too shrewd to be well liked.
H-4 or H-5 L-7 P-3	Bravery.

D-4 in combination with:

E-2 or E-3 G-1 or G-2 J-2 Hasty writing	Business ability.
C-4 or C-5 L-3 Q-1	A kind and considerate person who is tolerant and sympathetic.
Q-37 or Q-51 Punctuation carelessly done	A sure sign of absent-mindedness.
C-3 H-3B P-4	Arrogance and vanity.
J-3 M-1 Q-9 or Q-35 Hasty writing	Effusive and somewhat overpowering.
E-2 Q-19	This writer has a tendency to exaggerate.
L-13 or L-20 Q-35 Hasty writing	Hasty and impatient; fussy and irritable.

D-5
or
D-6   Extravagant, high strung and temperamental. Restless and somewhat spoiled. Apt to fly off the handle in a temper at the slightest provocation. Love of admiration and attention. These large writers nearly always have loud voices and are generally excellent entertainers. They love grandeur and display and are usually egotistical. They are generous, courageous and enthusiastic.

D-7   Erratic and abnormal. Love of grandeur and superlatives. Loud and long talker. Writing this size or larger can show almost anything from a jolly entertainer to a megalomaniac and sadist. There is nothing definite about it except that it is *abnormal*.

Spacing Between the Lines

SPACING *of lines shows clearness of thought and the reverse, since it is obvious that the more tangled up a line is with the line above or below, the more tangled up mentally is the writer. Just as obvious is the sign of extravagance or stinginess. Be sure to note whether the lines are evenly or unevenly spaced.*

E-1   A muddle-headed person whose thoughts keep getting mixed up with themselves. If the writing is very jumbled and tangled up, feeblemindedness is indicated. If there is no great entanglement of lines, we have a general lack of self-control and reserve together with a healthy economy which, in time, will lead to stinginess.

E-2   Clear and logical thinker. If the spacing is even or nearly even throughout, it shows an extrovert with self-confidence and a well-balanced mind (provided C-1 or C-2 are not present). If the spacing is uneven throughout we have a chatty and somewhat gullible person.

In combination with:

M-2
Q-3   }   Extremely talkative.
Q-9

C-4   }   "One of the boys." A joiner and a "regular
H-3A   fellow." He makes friends easily but is no
J-3   }   heavyweight mentally. Just a good guy.

E-3   A good organizer and executive. An excellent judge of character and a fine sense of justice is shown here. Love of luxury is also indicated. If the spacing is even throughout, he has firmly rooted ideas and convictions. These writers are nearly always interested in cultural subjects and are frequently patrons of the arts.

F

Margins

THE WIDTH *of margins shows culture, aestheticism and sense of values or the lack of them. Margins also reveal self-consciousness and extravagance. A very wide* LEFT *margin shows a somewhat impractical person of culture and refinement with a deep appreciation for the best in art and music. Narrow* LEFT *margins show the reverse. No* LEFT *margin at all shows a practical nature, a wholesome economy and a general lack of good taste in the arts. A very wide* RIGHT *margin shows a person afraid to face reality, over-sensitive to the future and generally a poor mixer. A very narrow* RIGHT *margin shows the reverse. Margins that grow wider at the bottom show inability to save money as well as haste and impatience. Margins that grow narrower at the bottom show the reverse. An all-round wide margin both left and right, shows a person of extremely delicate sensibilities with love of color and form; one who holds aloof from the multitude and lives in his own dream world of beauty and form. Such a writer is highly impractical and has little desire to mix with others.*

F-1
or
F-2   A good wholesome economy and a practical nature.

In combination with:

C-5	A "low-brow" and proud of it. He cares little
D-4	for "long hair" music or any other cultural
E-1	subject. He just wants to be alone to read
H-3C or H-4	the comics or listen to soap operas.
J-1	Thrift.

F-3   A somewhat impractical person with great self-respect and a slight self-consciousness. Apt to be a bit shy at times.

F-4   High aesthetic sense and love of the best in art, music and literature.
or   Love of color and color combinations. Artistic and somewhat imprac-
F-5   tical. Self-conscious and very fussy about small things.

The Shape of Small Letters—Garlands

SMALL m's *and n's that are sharply pointed at the tops show aggressiveness and energy especially if the writing is hurriedly written with the letters only half formed. If the letters are pointed at the base as shown in G-1, it indicates a sarcastic, stubborn and irritable nature. It may be set down as a general rule that the more sharply pointed the* m's *and n's are at the tops, the more energetic and aggressive is the writer, providing, of course, that the script is hastily written and the thickness of the letters is greater than H-1 or H-2. If the* m's *and n's are rounded at the tops we have just the opposite. Such a writer is docile and peace-loving, seldom doing things on his own initiative. If the* m's *and n's are very rounded at the tops the writer is apt to be totally lacking in ambition, lazy and indolent. You will have to look very closely in examining the sharpness or roundedness of the* m's *and n's. It might be a good idea to use a magnifying glass.*

G-1   If the writing is hasty with some letters only half formed, we have a person who is a "live wire" both mentally and physically (provided H-1 and H-2 are absent). He does things and gets things done and never lets the grass grow under his feet. He is the type of person who is always thinking up schemes and seeing them through. He is a go-getter, quick and active in both mind and body. If the writing is slowly done with nearly all the letters legible and some carefully formed, we have a bright and alert individual who lacks the necessary push to do things and get them done. Such writers are active more mentally than they are physically. Hasty G-1 writers, in the absence of H-1 or H-2, will nearly always take a chance on a new venture.

G-2   If the writing is hasty with some letters only half formed, we have a person who is moderately aggressive. It really is not in his nature, and he is aggressive only when he has to be. Though not lazy in any sense of the word, he has a certain docile streak in his make-up which keeps him from taking chances or taking the initiative. If the writing is slowly done with nearly all the letters legible, these qualities are emphasized. The G-2 writer may be successful in his business or profession, but he is very apt to miss opportunities because he won't take a chance.

G-3   Docile and peace-loving. Lacking in push and aggressiveness. This is particularly true if H-1 or H-2 are present. This writer will seldom start anything by himself and will never take the initiative in anything. If the writing is very slow and all the letters are carefully formed, we have a writer who is extremely cautious and somewhat lazy and unambitious. A lack of spontaneity is clearly indicated in this G-3 script.

G-4   This is known as the GARLAND, or letter connections very clearly rounded at the bottom. You will see it often to a greater or lesser degree, and when you see it you may be sure that the writer is adaptable, receptive and responsive. He is nearly always peace-loving and good natured and will avoid all arguments and fights. Though cultured and generally fond of the best in music and art, he is no great hustler, for he is inclined to take the line of least resistance most of the time. He has a warm and affectionate nature and is kind and tolerant. Very often, if the writing is hasty and "flows along" at a fast pace, these garlands show creative ability in music, literature and art. Such is the writing of musicians and concert vocalists, particularly if the script is in the D-5 class.

G-5   This is known as the ARCADE, or letters arched at the top like the entrance to the great cathedrals of Europe. The specimen is exaggerated in its deliberate slowness but the arched *m's* give you the idea of the "arched roof" of the small letters. You will see this writing often to a greater or lesser degree, and when you do you may be sure that the writer is rather reserved, difficult to know well and generally interested in structural art like architecture and even sculpture. Arcade writers may seem to be informal in their manner and actions, but they are really quite the opposite. They would much rather be alone with Nature and the great outdoors than with groups of people. They are often pretentious and affected and nearly always restrained and reserved. Do not confuse this G-5 with G-3. The very rounded tops of the *m's* and *n's* are quite different from the dull tops shown in D-3. The arcade writer is seldom lazy or indolent.

The Thickness of the Letters

USUALLY, *the heavier the pressure or the thickness of the writing, the more self-confidence and "push" and energy the writer will have, and conversely. Thick writing nearly always shows a very healthy development of the physical senses with a love of physical pleasures. If heavy writing is also hastily done, it shows a person of great energy and perhaps, creative ability.*

NOTE: It will be very difficult for the novice to judge thickness in the handwriting that is done with a ballpoint pen or a Parker 51. These pens always make the same width of line so the thickness of the writing will not vary as it does with the usual pens. In this case you will have to use your own judgment as to the darkness or lightness of the lines. If they are light, you can put the writer in the H-3 class; if dark, the writer is in the H-4 class. If the script is not made with a Parker 51 or a ballpoint pen, you may be sure of getting a more accurate analysis by referring to the H numbers and their combinations below.

It is extremely important to note whether the pressure varies in the different words. To determine this you may need a magnifying glass. If the pressure varies noticeably, thin for a few letters and then very thick for the next few in a given word, it may show some undesirable traits. This does not apply to writing that is shaded evenly and naturally.

H-1 This extremely thin writing shows a lack of energy. It reveals a quiet, modest personality, non-aggressive and somewhat shy. This writer is kind and tender and never tries to dominate or to make an impression.

In combination with:

L-9   The timid soul.

Q-51   Aspiration.

H-1 in combination with:

D-2 G-1 or G-2 }	Mentally alert with excellent concentration but lacking in aggressiveness and push. A bit too modest for his own good.
C-3 or C-4	Tender, kind and considerate of others.

H-2   Here is a writer with spirituality and refinement. His tastes and manners are quiet and modest and his whole personality is simple, unassuming and unaffected. His general character is the same as the H-1 writer to a lesser degree; that is, he is not quite so shy and slightly more aggressive.

H-3   This is the average thickness but the analysis must be done with care and, possibly, a magnifying glass. Examine it closely to see if the letters are evenly thick throughout or if they are shaded (thicker on the down strokes than they are on the up strokes). If the letters are all evenly thick, we have H-3A; if they are shaded, we have H-3B; and if they are shaded for effect with large flourishes for capitals, we have H-3C.

H-3A	This is the average thickness and means nothing by itself.
H-3B	This naturally shaded writing shows an insistent nature and a distinctive personality.
H-3C	This "beautiful" writing with all the flourishes and affected shading shows a rather commonplace person who lacks ambition, an over-conventional type who would be a good show-card writer at an amusement park or a very small-time clerk. He is a stickler for conventional form and fads and has little distinctive personality.

H-4   Materialism and sensuousness. A strong will with perseverance, diligence, resoluteness and severity. This writer has great self-confidence and usually dominates a situation. Love of eating and other physical pleasures. Love of outdoor sports and competition where physical skill and strength are involved.

H-4 in combination with:

       Q-16   Athletic ability and physical strength.

H-5
and
H-6   The same characteristics as H-4 to a much greater degree.

H-7   This smeary and pasty writing is dangerous, particularly if it is slowly done in the H-3 class. The pressure is uneven, some of the letters in the same word are thick and others thin. The edges of the strokes are coarse and feathery and the script is dirty and smudgy. Put the character of the writer down as totally bad, provided it is his natural script and a bad pen is not responsible. He is coarse and vulgar with marked tendencies toward sexual perversion. Sometimes these writers are loud and boastful and other times they are sly and evasive. They can never be trusted. This dirty, smudgy and feather-edge writing that continually varies in pressure is common among criminals. If you ever run across writing like this and you are sure that the pen or the ink has nothing to do with the smears and blotches and uneven pressure, beware of the writer. Other examples of H-7 are given on page 101.

J

Compressed or Extended Writing

Just as one might extend his hand and come forward in greeting an-other while someone else would draw back and "crawl into his shell" under the same circumstances, so extended writing shows friendliness and warmth while compressed writing shows the reverse.

J-1   Here is a poor mixer; a person who would rather be alone than with a crowd. Such a writer is inhibited and shy and possibly has an inferiority complex. He never lets himself go and is always restraining himself from doing what he wants to do. He is not apt to have many good friends because he is inclined to be suspicious, jealous and overcautious. He is usually tactful. In combination with G-5 these characteristics are intensified.

J-2   This is the average writing and means nothing by itself.

J-3   Spontaneity, initiative, courage and daring. A good mixer, a good teller of stories, a good talker and entertainer and a good, all-round fellow. If the writing is exceptionally extended it shows a spendthrift and a possible gambler. The J-3 writer is often apt to be careless and impatient.

Even and Uneven Small Letters

THE EVENNESS *of the small letters shows the consistency, sincerity and conscientiousness of the writer. If the letters are all the same height or about the same height, it is a sure indication of dependability and a strong desire always to do the right thing. In combination with M-1 or M-2 and A-1 it is the writer's unqualified recommendation for an excellent character—honest, straightforward and truthful. Unevenness in small letters, letters that constantly vary in size to a marked degree, shows a decided changeableness and shiftiness. Such writers are not always dependable and reliable. Writing where the small letters approach a wavy, thready line that is illegible (K-4) shows a writer that is highly intelligent, somewhat crafty and extremely shrewd.*

K-1   A changeable nature; a moody person sometimes lacking in emotional stability. This writer is not consistent and may not be reliable at all times.

In combination with:

A-2
D-2   }   Versatility.

Q-44 or Q-49   A scatterbrain. One who simply can't make up his mind. He is always jumping from one scheme to another.

A-2
M-4   }   Deceit and dishonesty. Watch out for this writer.

A-2
M-4 or M-5   }   A criminal who will stop at nothing. Anything can happen with this writer, from stealing to cold-blooded murder. It is doubtful if you will ever see this filthy combination outside of our prisons.
H-7

H-7
Q-16   }   Coarseness, vulgarity, gluttony. No intellectual or moral stability. A perfect example of what to avoid.
Q-72

K-2   This writer is reliable and trustworthy as well as painstaking and conscientious.

In combination with:

A-1
M-1 or M-2   }   Honesty, sincerity, truthfulness.

D-1
Q-31   }   Great concentration and unlimited painstaking. This writer has an enormous capacity for details and little regard for time. He will work for hours on end to solve what may seem to us the most insignificant problems A perfectionist.

C-4
H-3C
P-4   }   An egotistical stuffed shirt.

K-3   This writer can drive a hard bargain. He is extremely shrewd, discreet, diplomatic and subtle and is not always sincere.

K-4   The same as K-3 only more so. He will adapt himself to almost any situation where he can gain, although he is not necessarily dishonest. This writing will be found among shrewd diplomats and opportunists.

Finals

1. Self-sufficiency. A prudent, careful and generally reticent nature. Inclined to be selfish.
2. Reticent and somewhat retiring. These writers hate to be conspicuous and seldom "hold forth" in a group.
3. These writers are generous and liberal. They are nearly always considerate of the feelings of others.
4. Generously extravagant. Critical and intolerant with decided and fixed opinions.
5. Self-consciousness. Sometimes this shows an interest in the mystical and a tendency to "live in the clouds." Nearly always impractical.
6. Protectiveness. Willingness and desire to shield others.
7. These writers will nearly always take a chance when confronted with danger. They are brave and daring, especially if H-4 and C-6 are present.
8. Somewhat unsympathetic, self-centered and selfish.
9. Timidity. In combination with Q-49 this is apt to show cowardice.
10. Obstinacy. Often an indication of temper.
11. Very strong likes and dislikes. Inclined to be intolerant.
12. Great tenacity of purpose. Stubborn and steadfast nature. These writers are friendly and courteous and generally outspoken.
13. These writers will not stand for any criticism. They are nearly always perverse and opinionated in their ideas.
14. The same characteristics as indicated in L-3.
15. Clublike or snakelike finals are always an indication of brutality, slyness
& and other very undesirable traits. Avoid these writers but be sure your
16. analysis is correct.
17. Kindliness, friendliness and warmth of personality. These writers are usually versatile.
18. Great determination is shown here together with curiosity and suspicion.
19. A very sensitive writer who is rather naïve and unsophisticated. Good imagination and love of poetry is indicated.
20. A matter-of-fact nature. Calm and not easily aroused to any degree of enthusiasm.
21. Selfishness.
22. Vanity and pretension. Somewhat impressed with his own importance.

M

Tops of *A's* and *O's* Open or Closed

OPEN AND *closed a's and o's are similar to the open and closed mouth. The person who tells most of the things he knows and has nothing to hide must have his mouth open or partly open in the telling just as he must have his a's and o's open or partly open in the writing. A person who can keep a secret has to "keep his mouth closed" just as he keeps his a's and o's closed. When secrets become extremely important and might give the writer or his friend away, the mouth must be "locked or tied up" and the same applies to the tightly knotted a's and o's. There can be no other psychological reason for a person knotting his letters closed. He must be naturally secretive. If all, or nearly all the letters in a given specimen are tightly knotted and the writing gives the appearance of being "knitted with a knitting needle," it is not a good sign. Small a's and o's and other letters that are broken at the base, resembling stencil letters, show hypocrisy, cunning and deceit.*

M-1 Frankness, truthfulness and sincerity. If the tops of the *a's* and *o's* are
or   wide open, the writer is much too frank for his own good; he is totally
M-2 lacking in tact.

In combination with:

Q-3 and Q-49   Gossip.

M-3 This writer is close-mouthed and doesn't tell all he knows. He is tactful and diplomatic and can keep a secret very well.

M-4 Extreme secretiveness. Slyness and craftiness if all the letters are knotted tight all the time and the letter *s* is tied in a knot at the base.

M-5 This is the danger signal of graphology. Be sure the small letters are broken at the *base* or that they resemble stencil letters before you pronounce them M-5. This writing is rare but when you do find it you may be sure that the writer is not to be trusted or depended upon in any way. He is cunning and crafty and will steal and lie to suit his own ends. No matter how nice and attractive he may appear, just watch your step. Don't jump to conclusions with this writing, make sure that the small *a's* and *o's* and other letters are broken continually at the *bottom* or that they look as though they were stenciled.

Connected Letters

CONNECTED *letters show the ability of the writer to think logically and to reason things through to their conclusions without sliding over the many details. Disconnected letters show just the reverse. These writers nearly always act on their hunches and seldom stop to think things through. They invariably jump at conclusions and are extremely intuitive, a characteristic which is more feminine than masculine. If the words in a specimen of handwriting are connected to one another, as shown in N-4, you may be sure that the writer is stubborn and thorough and sometimes a bit opinionated.*

N-1   A practical, logical and prudent person. A natural reasoner who never makes up his mind hastily on matters of importance. The N-1 writer is usually argumentative and generally has a one-track mind. He is difficult to convince once his mind is made up.

In combination with:

E-2
G-1 or G-2   } Aggressiveness; business ability. A good law-
H-3   yer or business executive.

G-3   } An easy-going, plodding type of mind with
Q-25   very little imagination or creative ability.

C-3
D-5   } Overdeveloped ego. Too conceited for his
P-4   own good.

N-2   This writer is creative. He arrives at decisions hastily and instinctively. He has plenty of imagination and is generally known as an "idea man." Some of his hunches may be wrong, but not many of them. He is much more interesting than the N-1 writer because he is inventive, imaginative, witty and often much quicker on the trigger, sizing up a situation almost instantly. His likes and dislikes are formed on first impressions, and he is difficult to deceive, particularly if Q-72 is present. Most original thinkers write the N-2 script. It is the writing of people with imagination.

N-3   Very seldom practical, this writer lives in a world of ideals and fairy tales. He is somewhat inconsistent and moody at times, particularly when his dreams don't materialize. Many poets and artists write this script.

N-4   Stubborn and obstinate. Cannot be shaken from his fixed and decided opinions. Usually a stickler for principles and generally conservative in manner and dress.

The Capital Letters

P-1 Humility.

P-2 Simplicity of tastes; modesty.

P-3 Self-respect, self-confidence and pride.

P-4 Conceit. If the capitals are lavishly flourished, we have affectation, vanity, pretentiousness and gross conceit.

Q

Letters Separately

Q-1   Pride and sensitivity.

Q-2   Originality. Distinctive personality. Fixed opinions and set ideas.

Q-3   Vivacity, chattiness.

Q-4   Culture and good taste. Creative ability.

Q-5   Modesty and considerable dignity.

Q-6   Shrewdness.

Q-7   Flirtatiousness and gaiety. Social aggressiveness.

Q-8   Imaginative and cultured. Analytical and sensitive.

Q-9   Sensitive and susceptibility to flattery.

Q-10   Taciturnity, quietness.

Q-11   Eccentricity and pretentiousness.

Q-12   Obstinacy. Firm convictions and strong prejudices.

Q-13   Poetic tastes. A simple and child-like personality.

Q-14   Austerity.

Q-15   Secretiveness.

Q-16   Love of outdoor sports. Practical "down-to-earth" personality.

Q-17   Physical weakness.

Q-18   Fluency of thought, a quick mind.

Q-19   Exaggeration and egoism.

Q-20   Taste for mathematics and figures.

Q-21   Clannishness and selfishness.

Q-22   Taste for literature and other cultural subjects. Good talker.

Q-23   Aggressiveness. A definite sarcasm is indicated here.

Q-24   Friendliness and amiability.

Q-25   Lacking in imagination. Humility.

Q-26   Imagination and keen vision. Lives in a world of thought not things.

Q-27   Precise and exact nature. Extremely careful. A perfectionist.

Q-28   Somewhat impulsive and intuitive.

Q-29   Curiosity.

Q-30   Caution and care. Procrastination and hesitation.

Q-31   Concentration, precision and good judgment. Excellent at detail work.

Q-32   Strong will with a materialistic nature.

Q-33   Weak will. Timidity. Easily swayed by opinions of others.

Q-34   Self-consciousness and somewhat egotistical.

Q-35   Vivacity, enthusiasm, energy, irritability and sometimes, worry.

Q-36   Humor, wit.

Q-37   Carelessness and absent-mindedness.

Q-38   Easily adaptable to circumstances.

Q-39   Not easily adaptable to circumstances.

Q-40   Alert and alive. Quick, active mind.

Q-41   Somewhat dull and lazy type.

Q-42   Not easily moved to change in ways and habits.

Q-43   Enthusiasm, energy, liveliness.

Q-44   Hesitation, caution and procrastination.

Q-45   Quick decisions. Not thorough. Apt to rush to get things done quickly

Q-46   Impulsiveness and some creative ability.

Q-47   Lack of aggressiveness. Weak will.

Q-48   Firmness and determination. Self-assurance and will power.

Q-49   Same as Q-47, only more so.

Q-50   Kindness and a tendency toward humility.

Q-51   Imagination and creative ability. Builds "air castles" and is irritable.

Q-52   Same as Q-37.

Q-53 Desire for self-improvement.

Q-54 Obstinate and contrary.

Q-55 Critical about everyone except himself. Opinionated and stubborn.

Q-56 Ability to mimic.

Q-57-8 Tenacity. Sometimes indicates greed and envy.

Q-59 A rather matter-of-fact nature with a dry sense of humor.

Q-60 A matter-of-fact nature.

Q-61 Good repartee and some sarcasm.

Q-62 Temper which grows gradually.

Q-63 Sudden temper which explodes and dies down.

Q-64 Unusual self-assurance. Very decided opinions.

Q-65 Practical joker.

Q-66 A show-off and egoist.

Q-67 Very sensitive nature. Feelings easily hurt. Won't take criticism.

Q-68 Jealousy and selfishness.

Q-69 Lack of self-confidence.

Q-70 Credulity.

Q-71 A skeptic.

Q-72 Vulgarity and coarseness. A very undesirable person.

Q-73 Independence and a healthy self-respect.

Q-74 Opinionated and arrogant.

Q-75 Lack of tact.

Q-76 Simplicity, neatness and orderliness.

Q-77 Wastefulness. Diplomacy and finesse.

Q-78 Kindness and friendliness.

Q-79 Timidity and lack of self-confidence.

Q-80 Creative and artistic. Original and cultured.

INDEX TO CHARACTERISTICS

NOTE: This index contains combinations of items in this book. All these combinations must be present in the undesirable characteristics and at least fifty per cent of them must be present in all others.

A

Absent-mindedness
Q-37 or Q-52
Accuracy
Letters carefully made
Q-31
Acquisitiveness
J-1
L-12 or L-13
Adaptability
Q-38
Aesthetic
C-3
D-2 or D-3
F-4 or F-5
Q-8
Affection
C-5 or C-6
H-2
K-2
Aggressiveness
G-1
Hasty writing
C-4 or C-5
Agreeableness
G-4
H-2 or H-3
J-3
Q-24
Ambition
B-1 or B-2
C-4 or C-5
G-1 or G-2
Hasty writing
Animation
G-1
Q-28 or Q-43
Hasty writing

Argumentativeness
E-2 (uneven spacing)
N-3 or N-4
Q-3 or Q-23
Arrogance
C-3
H-3B
P-4
Artistic Tastes
E-3
F-4
Q-78 or Q-79
Athletic Ability
H-4 or H-5
Q-16
Avarice
C-2 or C-3
J-1
L-12 or L-13

B

Bashfulness
H-1
J-1
P-1 or P-2
L-9
Boldness
D-5 or D-6
H-4 or H-5
J-3
Q-23
Bravery
H-4 or H-5
L-7
Broad-mindedness
E-3

Brusqueness
  D-5 or D-6
  H-4 or H-5
  P-4
  Q-39
Brutality
  A-2
  C-1 or C-2
  H-4 or H-5
  L-15
  M-4
  Writing not hasty
Business Ability
  C-4 or C-5
  E-3
  G-1
  N-1 or N-4
  Hasty writing

C

Calmness
  G-2 (slow writing)
  H-1 or H-2
  Q-50
Carelessness
  Q-37 or Q-52
Caution
  C-3
  Q-30 or Q-44
  Slow, careful writing
Clannishness
  J-1
  Q-21
Coarseness
  H-7
  A-2
  M-4
  K-1
  Q-72
Conceit
  P-4
Concentration
  D-1 or D-2

E-3
Q-31
Conscientiousness
  K-2
Conventionality
  C-4
  H-3B
Coquetry
  Q-7
Cowardice
  H-1
  L-9
  Q-49
Creative Ability
  D-1 or D-2
  E-3
  N-1 or N-2
  Q-4 or Q-8
  Q-26
Critical Ability
  C-3
  D-3
  E-3
  L-4
Cruelty
  H-7
  L-15 or L-16
Culture
  F-3 or F-4
  Q-8 or Q-78
Cunning
  G-1
  H-4 or H-5
  K-1 or K-4
  L-12
  M-4

D

Deceit
  A-2
  K-1
  M-4

Dependability
A-1
C-5 or C-6
M-2
Depression
B-4 or B-5
Determination
B-2
G-1
L-7
Q-47 or Q-48
Diligence
H-5 or H-6
Diplomacy
K-3 or K-4
Dishonesty
A-2
K-1
M-4
    or
H-7 or M-5

E

Emotional nature
C-5 or C-6
Energy
G-1
Q-28 or Q-35
Hasty writing
Enthusiasm
B-2
G-1 or G-2
Q-26 or Q-35 or Q-53
Very hasty writing
Exaggeration
D-5 or D-6
Q-19
Extravagance
E-3
F-4 or F-5
Few words in large space

F

Fastidiousness
J-2
Q-35
Punctuation carefully placed
Finesse
K-3 or K-4
Firmness
H-4
Q-48
Flattery
C-5 or C-6
Q-9
Flirtatiousness
Q-7
Frankness
A-1
K-2
M-1 or M-2
Friendliness
C-4 or C-5
G-4
Q-24
Fussiness
J-2
Q-35
Punctuation carefully placed

G

Gaiety
B-2
C-4
D-5
J-3
Q-7 or Q-61
Generosity
C-4 or C-5
D-4 or D-5
L-3 or L-4
Gluttony
Q-72

Gossip
M-1
Q-3 or Q-49

H

Hastiness
Hasty writing
Q-43 or Q-46
Honesty
A-1
K-2
M-1 or M-2
Humility
P-1
Humor
L-12
Q-36, 57, 58 or 61
Hypocrisy
M-5

I

Idealism
B-2
H-1
N-2 or N-3
Imagination
N-2
Q-8 or Q-26
Impulsiveness
N-2 or N-3
Q-43 or Q-46
Incredulity
Q-71
Independence
A-1
L-4 or L-7
Q-47 or Q-73
Indolence
C-3
G-3 (slow writing)
Q-41

Initiative
G-1
Hasty writing
Intuition
N-2
Irritability
Q-35 or Q-43
Hasty writing

J

Jealousy
C-5 or C-6
L-10
Q-1 or Q-68
Judgment
C-3
D-2 or D-3
E-3
N-1
Q-31

L

Laziness
C-3
G-3 (slow writing)
Literary tastes
Q-22
Logic
N-1
Loquaciousness
E-2
M-2
Q-3 or Q-9
Loyalty
A-1
H-1 or H-2
Only one form used for each letter

M

Materialism
H-4, 5, or 6
Q-32

Pride
P-3
Q-1
Procrastination
Q-30 or Q-44

Q

Quarrelsomeness
E-2 (uneven spacing)
H-5
Q-3 or Q-23
Q-35

R

Refinement
H-1 or H-2
J-2
Q-4
Reserve
G-5
M-3
Reticence
L-2
M-3

S

Sagacity
E-3
G-1
N-2
Sarcasm
G-1 (pointed at bottom)
Q-23
Secretiveness
M-3
Q-15
Self-confidence
H-5 or H-6
Q-48

Self-consciousness
C-1 or C-2
F-4
Selfishness
C-1 or C-2
L-1 or L-8
Q-68
Sensitiveness
C-5 or C-6
H-1
Q-1 or Q-8
Q-9 or Q-67
Sensuousness
H-5 or H-6
Q-64
Sentimentality
C-6
Needless underscoring and
use of punctuation
Shrewdness
K-4
Q-6
Simplicity of taste
H-1 or H-2
P-2
Q-76 or Q-80
Sincerity
A-1
K-2
M-1 or M-2
Skepticism
Q-71
Slyness
A-2
M-4
Sociability
J-3
Q-38
Stubbornness
L-10
N-4
Q-12

certain chemicals will
the various materials
jewelry is made and is
ruin them. A hot metal
spilled on a ring or a

5

stairs for,

room. I f

address wh

through the

6

nd I am tired of it,
typbred, but country b
nd hope to spend th
st of my life in
ountry. Thanking

7

actually do publish th b
would can to wait unt
th manuscript) you will
f proposal we would mak

8

I will certainly
Mr Solomon as you
and will then comp
you. I will certain
too. glad to show th

9

nd Noll has'nt heard
her been with the dean
AM (with someone) bought
in 41 street near 3rd A
they will convert into a
ffice building, primaril
own use. Jerome showe
th drafting-room plan.
nd lighter and airy an

10

is the will of the
o to live ———— and i
the terms of freedon
nd self reserve.

11

~ y stress the
for you to use a
Yours truly

12

99

ANSWERS

To Handwriting Quiz

THE FIRST THING to do is look for the two thieves, and this is done by a close examination of all the specimens. It must be quite obvious that numbers 7 and 9 are abnormal writings. Note the uneven pressures and the muddy feather-edge script and you will see that it comes under the heading of H-7. These two writers are not to be trusted. The round G-5 writing in specimen 7 shows a rather lazy and dull type of mentality, a person who will deceive you at the drop of a hat. He is a slow, abnormal type who will lie and steal whenever he gets a chance, provided it is not too much effort. The other fellow, number 9, is a much more aggressive type of criminal . . . a vulgar, boastful, shrewd sneak who will stop at nothing to gain his objective. He is crafty and energetic and could have made an honest financial success of himself if he hadn't fallen into the wrong company and followed a career of crime. Note the extreme unevenness of the pressure and dirty, smeary appearance of the writing in general.

Having located the two thieves, let us try to find the other people mentioned in the problem.

The athlete is practically shouting at you from specimen 12. Here indeed is a perfect example of Q-16, showing love of outdoor sports and physical strength. Certainly the extra long down strokes on the *y's* in "you" and "yours" and the strong cross of the *t* in "truly" are very clear indications of physical strength and suggest an athletic person.

Now look at the small and intellectual script in specimen 10. Here we have the magnificent combination of characteristics C-3, D-2, G-2 and H-2. This is clearly the handwriting of a literary person . . . a creator and a writer of ability. Of all the specimens shown here, this is the only one which shows a novelist or creative writer . . . a person of extreme culture and originality with a keen imagination and good critical sense.

Now look at specimen 3. This C-2 slope shows an introvert, a person who is always inquiring into the whys and wherefores of life.

Specimen 11 is a fine example of H-5. Note the evenness and extreme thickness of this script and how different it is from specimen 7, with its uneven pressure. Number 11 clearly shows a person of unusual perseverance and great self-confidence . . . one who is more likely than any of the others to be a well-known public figure.

With the exception of specimen 4, which shows terrific energy and speed . . . a real wide-awake go-getter if ever there was one . . . there is nothing striking or outstanding about the rest of the specimens.

SAMPLES of H-7 and M-5

H-7

M-5

H-7 and M-5

H-7